Piano • Vocal

The Roar of the Greasepaint
- The Smell of the Crowd

ISBN: 978-0-634-01697-4

Musical Comedy Productions, Inc.

TRO The Richmond Organization

Hal•Leonard
CORPORATION

7777 W. BLUEMOUND RD. P.O. BOX 13819 MILWAUKEE, WI 53213

From the David Merrick-Bernard Delfont Production "THE ROAR OF THE GREASEPAINT - The Smell Of The Crowd"

The Beautiful Land

Words and Music by
LESLIE BRICUSSE and
ANTHONY NEWLEY

Tempo rubato

Verse

Red is the col - or of a pret - ty pil - lar box. Or - ange is an - y

or - ange on a tree. Yel - low's the col - or of a bag of

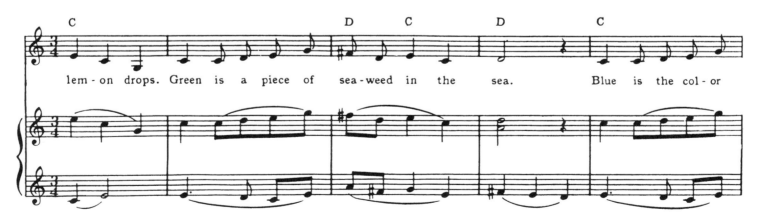

lem - on drops. Green is a piece of sea - weed in the sea. Blue is the col - or

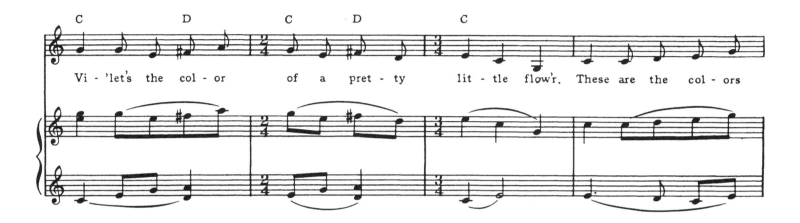

of the sky in sum-mer-time. In-di-go is a Si-a-mese cat's eyes.

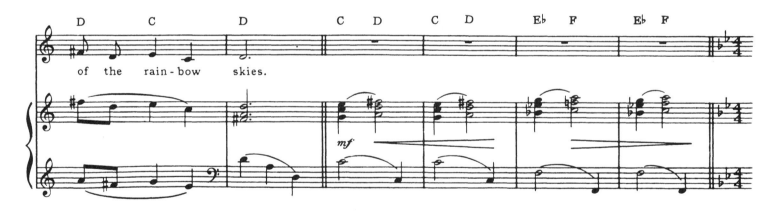

Vi-'let's the col-or of a pret-ty lit-tle flow'r. These are the col-ors

of the rain-bow skies.

Chorus - Moderately

There is a beau-ti-ful land where all your dreams come true, It's

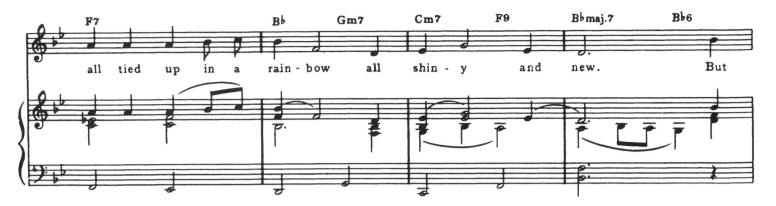

all tied up in a rain-bow all shin-y and new. But

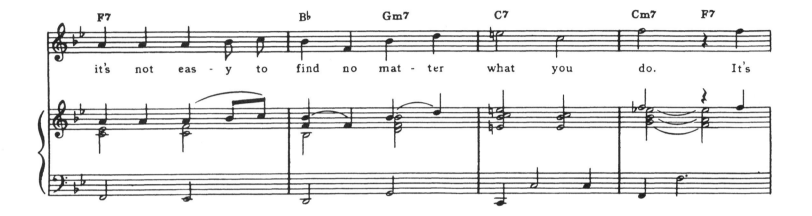

it's not eas-y to find no mat-ter what you do. It's

not on top of a moun-tain, or be-neath the deep blue sea, Or in

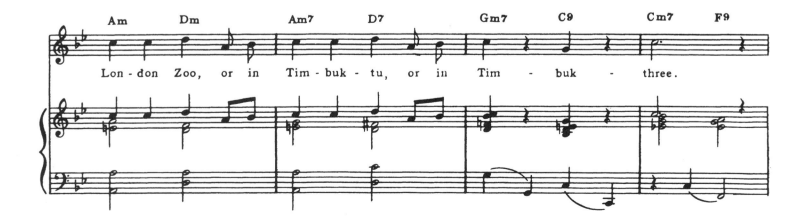

Lon-don Zoo, or in Tim-buk-tu, or in Tim - buk - three.

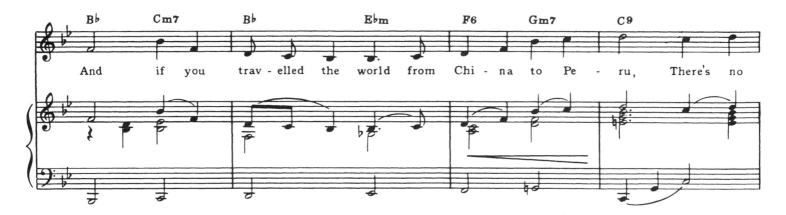

And if you trav-elled the world from Chi-na to Pe-ru, There's no

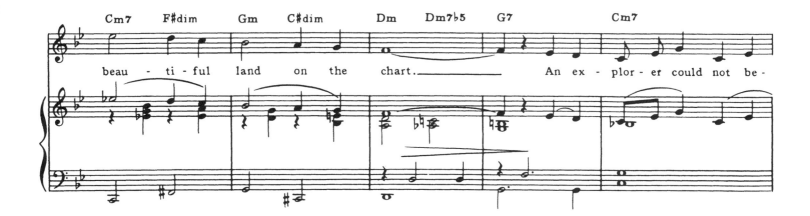

beau-ti-ful land on the chart. An ex-plor-er could not be-

gin to dis-cov-er its or-i-gin, For The Beau-ti-ful Land is

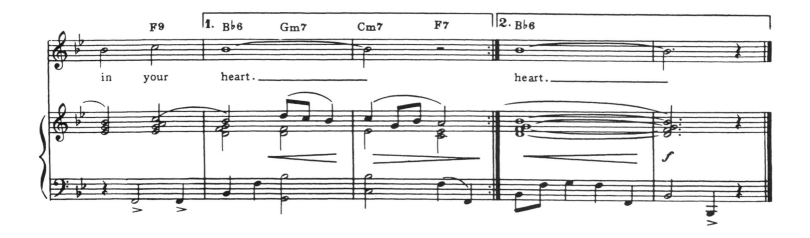

in your heart. heart.

From the David Merrick-Bernard Delfont Production "THE ROAR OF THE GREASEPAINT - The Smell Of The Crowd"

A Wonderful Day Like Today

Words and Music by
LESLIE BRICUSSE and
ANTHONY NEWLEY

sky was so blue, I in - stinc-tive-ly knew We were in for a won-der-ful day.___ As I

came through the door, As I told you be - fore, I was ter - ri - bly tempt - ed to say.

Chorus - Brightly

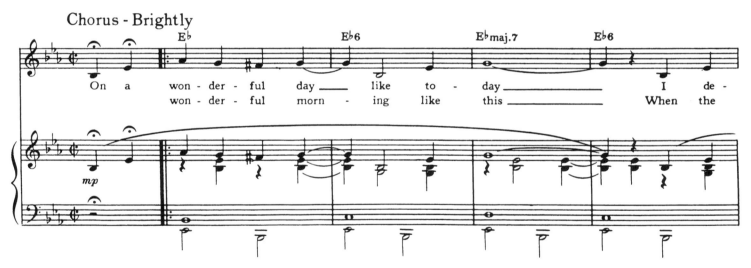

On a won - der - ful day ___ like to - day ___ I de -
won - der - ful morn - ing like this ___ When the

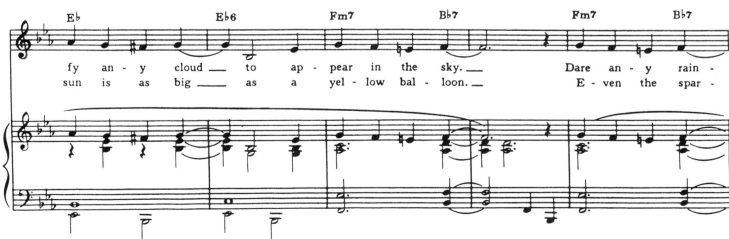

fy an - y cloud ___ to ap - pear in the sky.___ Dare an - y rain -
sun is as big ___ as a yel - low bal - loon.___ E - ven the spar -

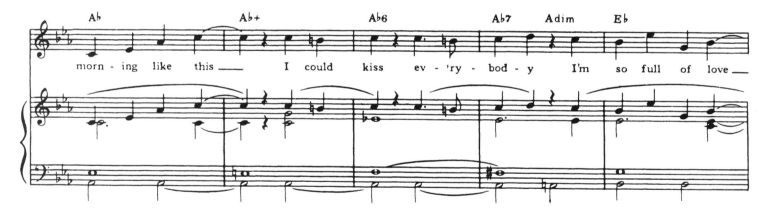

From the David Merrick-Bernard Delfont Production "THE ROAR OF THE GREASEPAINT - The Smell Of The Crowd"

It Isn't Enough

Words and Music by
LESLIE BRICUSSE and
ANTHONY NEWLEY

12

From the David Merrick-Bernard Delfont Production "THE ROAR OF THE GREASEPAINT - The Smell Of The Crowd"

Things To Remember

Words and Music by
LESLIE BRICUSSE and
ANTHONY NEWLEY

© Copyright 1965 (renewed), 2013 CONCORD MUSIC LTD., London, England
TRO MUSICAL COMEDY PRODUCTIONS, INC., New York, controls all rights for the U.S.A. and Canada
International Copyright Secured   *Made in U.S.A.*
All Rights Reserved Including Public Performance For Profit

Refrain, Moderately

1. There are so man-y things to re - mem - ber __ As you tra-vel the high-way of
2. (Please re -) mem-ber your grand-moth-er's birth-day __ And be proud of the flag at all

life. __ Like al - ways be kind to your hus-band — or, if you're a
times. __ Stand up for the Na - tion - al An - them. Sit down to re -

man, to your wife. __ You should nev - er shoot trout in Sep - tem - ber. __ You should
cite dirt - y rhymes. __ Al - ways hon - or your debts when you have to. __ And be

nev - er feed ba - bies on gin. __ Don't ev - er play po - ker on Sun - day —
hon - est un - less there's no need. __ Spend two hours a day with the Good Book —

un - less you are cer - tain to win! __ Don't go out of your way seek-ing
if you've noth-ing bet - ter to read. __ You must al - ways be pa - tient with

dan - ger __ Nev - er stand on a croc - o - dile's tail. __ Nev - er buy Lon - don
chil - dren, __ Though they jan - gle your nerves, it is true. __ If a child is a

Reprise lyrics

When I think of the era in which I was raised
And I see how the world's gone to waste,
I confess that I'm constantly shocked and amazed
At man's singular lack of good taste.
For taste is like justice, we live by her laws.
It's so easy to tell right from wrong.
Most people don't bother, most people are whores
And the few bores who do, don't for long.

REFRAIN
There are so many things to remember
From the deeply revered days of old,
When living was gentle and gracious
And working folk did as they're told.
They were wonderful days, I remember,
When a fella could live like a king
And children were working in coal mines
And life was a beautiful thing.
But the fortunes of mankind are changing
And things aren't what they were anymore
And although I'm in no way complaining,
By Harris and Tweed, I preferred it before.
Ah, but why speak of May in December.
When December is all that you'll get.
Man lives with a lingering ember
And while there are beautiful things to remember ,
The ugly things one should forget.

16

From the David Merrick-Bernard Delfont Production "THE ROAR OF THE GREASEPAINT-The Smell Of The Crowd"

Put It In The Book

Words and Music by
LESLIE BRICUSSE and
ANTHONY NEWLEY

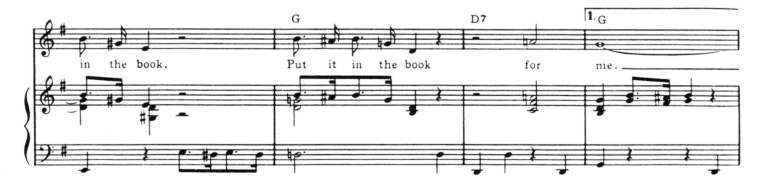

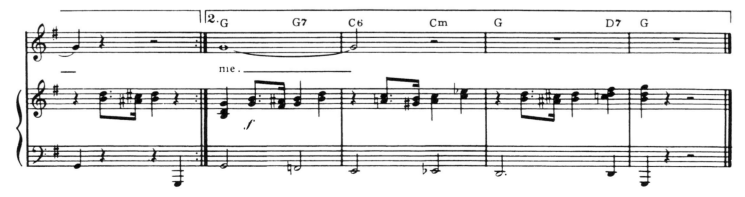

From the David Merrick-Bernard Delfont Production "THE ROAR OF THE GREASEPAINT–The Smell Of The Crowd"

With All Due Respect

Words and Music by
LESLIE BRICUSSE and
ANTHONY NEWLEY

Moderately but with rhythm

With all due re-
(With) all due re-

spect, sir, I'd like to say a word or three a-bout the way you're treat-ing me in
spect, sir, I think it's such a lib-er-ty the way you take it out on me. I'm

front of ev-'ry-one. ___ You say I lay a-bout and shirk. You must take me for
nev-er left a-lone. ___ You tell me I'm a lit-tle squirt. You treat me like a

such a jerk. 'Cause I do all the bleed-in' work and you have all the fun. ___
bit of dirt. I have-n't e-ven got a shirt to call me bleed-in' own! ___

Far be it from me, sir, To dare to carp or crit-i-cize, I just want you to re-al-ize I
I don't wish to be rude, sir, But ev-'ry-thing I do is wrong, You make me feel I don't be-long Be-

From the David Merrick-Bernard Delfont Production "THE ROAR OF THE GREASEPAINT-The Smell Of The Crowd"

This Dream

Words and Music by
LESLIE BRICUSSE and
ANTHONY NEWLEY

Moderately

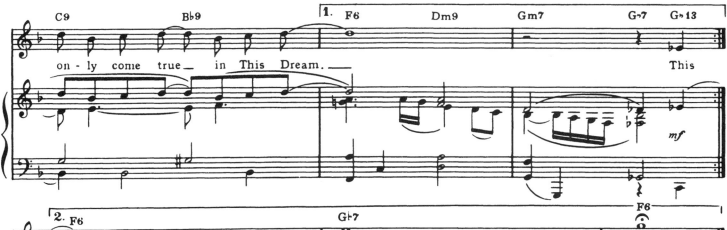

From the David Merrick - Bernard Delfont Production "THE ROAR OF THE GREASEPAINT - The Smell Of The Crowd"

Where Would You Be Without Me?

Words and Music by
LESLIE BRICUSSE and
ANTHONY NEWLEY

From the David Merrick - Bernard Delfont Production "THE ROAR OF THE GREASEPAINT - The Smell Of The Crowd"

Look At That Face

Words and Music by
LESLIE BRICUSSE and
ANTHONY NEWLEY

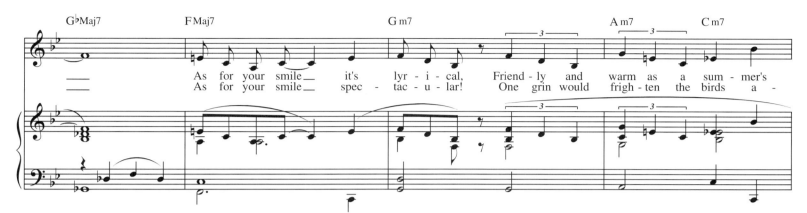

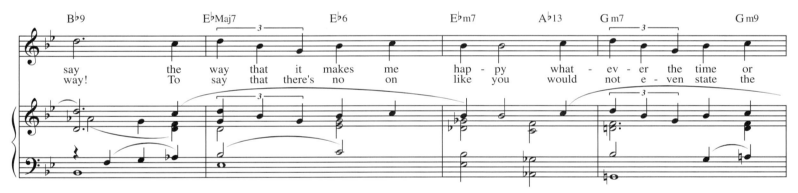

From the David Merrick–Bernard Delfont Production "THE ROAR OF THE GREASEPAINT - The Smell Of The Crowd"

My First Love Song

Words and Music by
LESLIE BRICUSSE and
ANTHONY NEWLEY

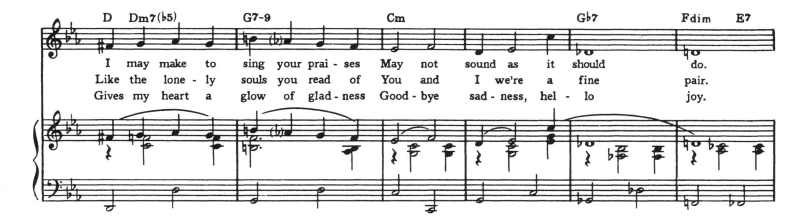

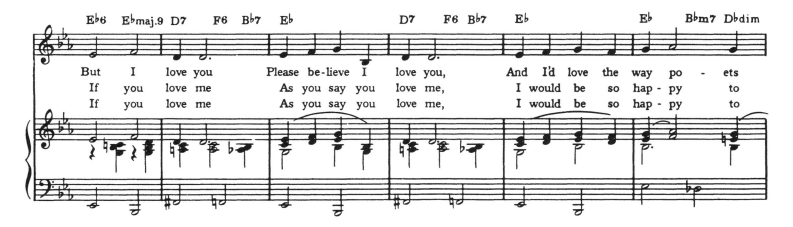

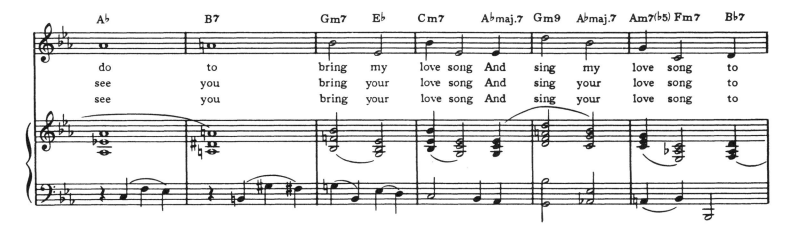

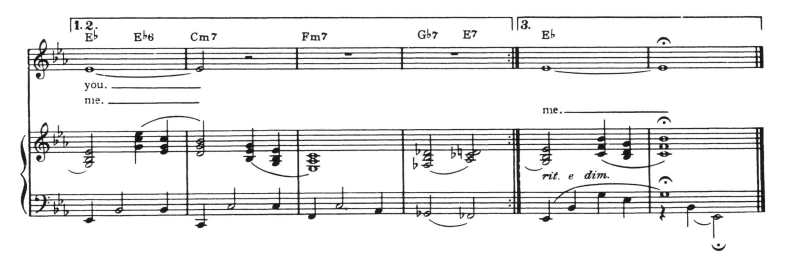

From the David Merrick-Bernard Delfont Production "THE ROAR OF THE GREASEPAINT-The Smell Of The Crowd"

The Joker

Words and Music by
LESLIE BRICUSSE and
ANTHONY NEWLEY

*Words as in stage production

From the David Merrick-Bernard Delfont Production "THE ROAR OF THE GREASEPAINT-The Smell Of The Crowd"

Who Can I Turn To
(When Nobody Needs Me)

Words and Music by
LESLIE BRICUSSE and
ANTHONY NEWLEY

Slowly with expression

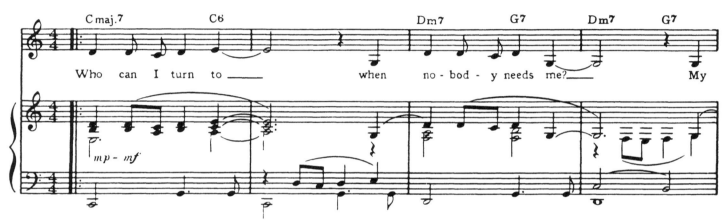

Who can I turn to ____ when no-bod-y needs me? ____ My

heart wants to know and so I must go where des-ti-ny leads me. ____ With

no star to guide me, _ and no-one be-side me, _ I'll go on my way, and

From the David Merrick-Bernard Delfont Production "THE ROAR OF THE GREASEPAINT - The Smell Of The Crowd"

That's What It Is To Be Young

Words and Music by
LESLIE BRICUSSE and
ANTHONY NEWLEY

From the David Merrick-Bernard Delfont Production "THE ROAR OF THE GREASEPAINT-The Smell Of The Crowd"

What A Man!

Words and Music by
LESLIE BRICUSSE and
ANTHONY NEWLEY

From the David Merrick-Bernard Delfont Production "THE ROAR OF THE GREASEPAINT - The Smell Of The Crowd"

Feeling Good

Words and Music by
LESLIE BRICUSSE and
ANTHONY NEWLEY

From the David Merrick-Bernard Delfont Production "THE ROAR OF THE GREASEPAINT-The Smell Of The Crowd

Nothing Can Stop Me Now!

Words and Music by
LESLIE BRICUSSE and
ANTHONY NEWLEY

Give ev-'ry-thing __ to it. I'll make all my dreams come true __
Go in and win __ a - gain. Get you all gone, you sky of grey __

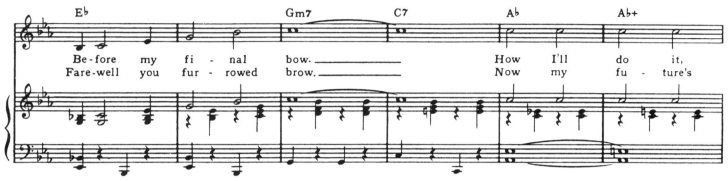

Be - fore my fi - nal bow. _____ How I'll do it,
Fare-well you fur - rowed brow. _____ Now my fu - ture's

who can say? _ But I know I will some day. _ Watch out,
crys - tal clear. _ No more woe for me to fear. _ I'm gon - na stand this

world, I'm on my way, _ Noth - ing Can Stop Me Now.
world up - on its ear, _ And I'll suc - ceed some

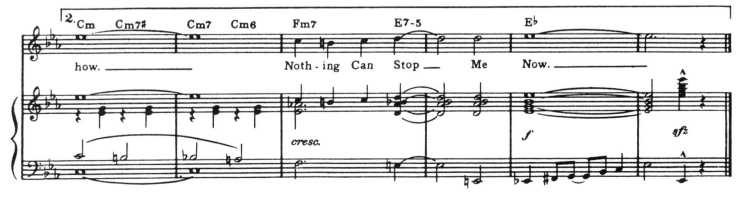

how. _____ Noth - ing Can Stop __ Me Now. _____

From the David Merrick-Bernard Delfont Production "THE ROAR OF THE GREASEPAINT-The Smell Of The Crowd"

My Way

Words and Music by
LESLIE BRICUSSE and
ANTHONY NEWLEY

Lively tempo

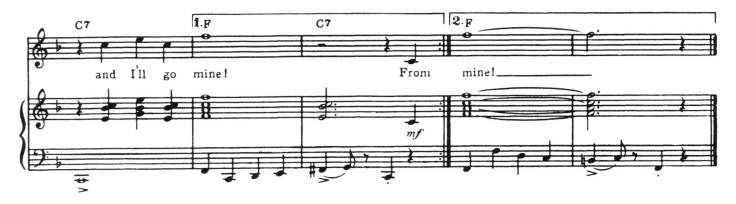

From the David Merrick-Bernard Delfont Production "THE ROAR OF THE GREASEPAINT - The Smell Of The Crowd"

Sweet Beginning

Words and Music by
LESLIE BRICUSSE and
ANTHONY NEWLEY

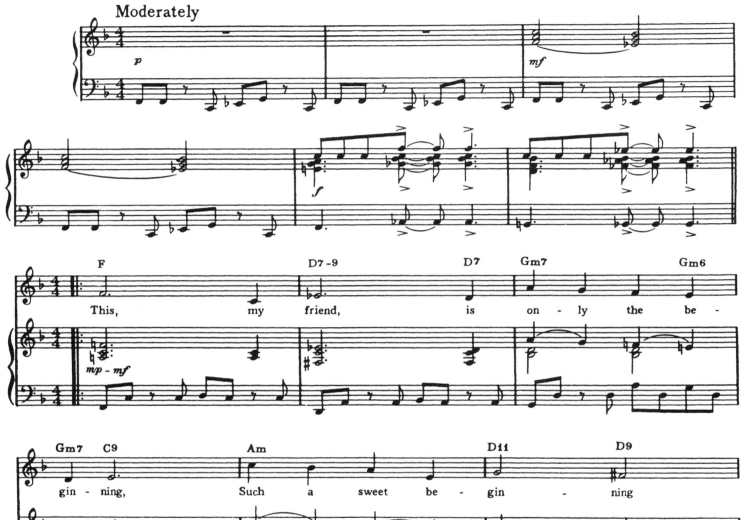

This, my friend, is on-ly the be-

gin - ning, Such a sweet be - gin - ning too. _____ Now, at

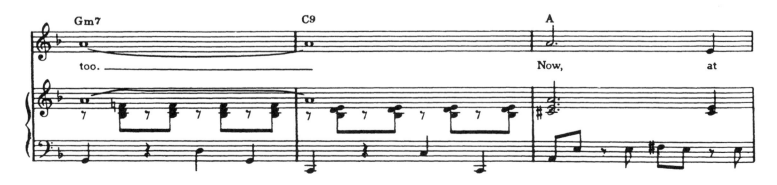

last, I see a chance of win - ning,

See a chance of break - ing through. _____

_____ Who can say? To -

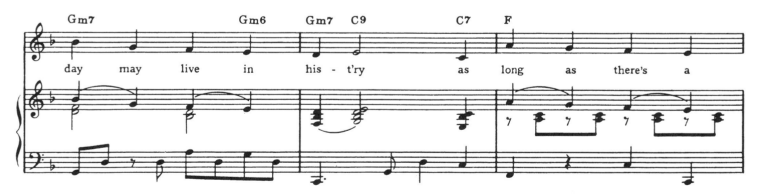

day may live in his - t'ry as long as there's a

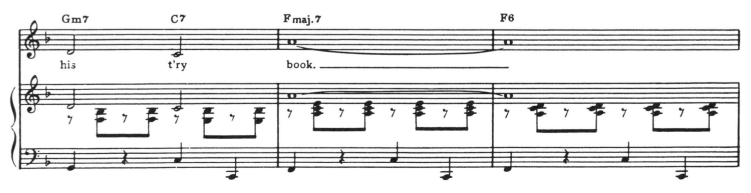

his t'ry book. _____

Yes - ter - day the world was still a

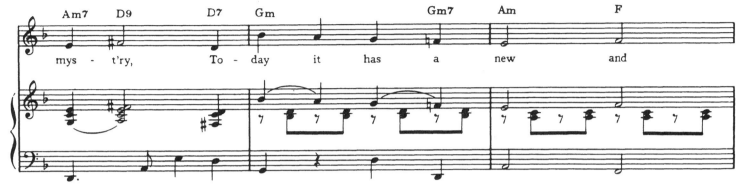

mys - t'ry, To - day it has a new and

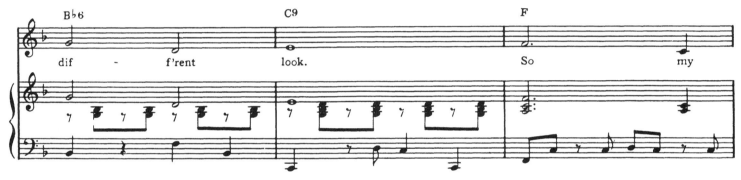

dif - f'rent look. So my

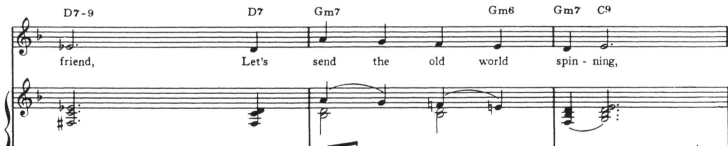

friend, Let's send the old world spin - ning,

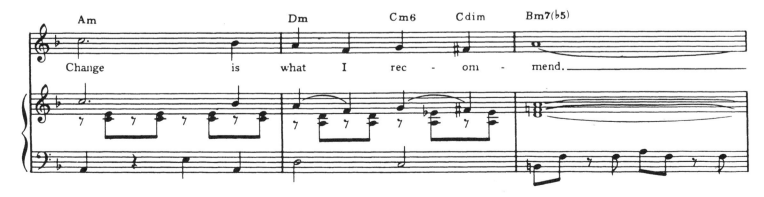

Change is what I rec - om - mend.

VOCAL SELECTIONS

HIGH SPIRITS – Hugh Martin and Timothy Gray

Forever and a Day • Home Sweet Heaven • I Know Your Heart • If I Gave You • Something Tells Me • Was She Prettier Than I? • You'd Better Love Me

OLIVER! REVISED EDITION – Lionel Bart

My Name • As Long As He Needs Me • Be Back Soon • I Shall Scream • Boy For Sale • That's Your Funeral • Consider Yourself • Food Glorious Food I'd Do Anything • It's a Fine Life • Oliver • Oom-Pah-Pah • Pick a Pocket or Two • Reviewing the Situation • Where Is Love? • Who Will Buy?

ONE TOUCH OF VENUS – Ogden Nash and Kurt Weill

Foolish Heart • How Much I Love You • I'm a Stranger Here Myself • One Touch of Venus • Speak Low • That's Him • The Trouble with Women • Very, Very, Very • Way Out West in Jersey • Westwind • Wooden Wedding

STOP THE WORLD – I Want to Get Off – Leslie Bricusse and Anthony Newley

All-American • Glorious Russian • Gonna Build a Mountain • I Wanna Be Rich • Lumbered • Meilinki Meilchik • Once in a Lifetime • Someone Nice Like You • Typically English • Typische Deutsche • What Kind of Fool Am I?

TAKING MY TURN – Will Holt and Gary William Friedman

Fine for the Shape I'm In • Good Luck to You • I Am Not Old • It Still Isn't Over • Pick More Daisies • Taking My Turn • This Is My Song • Two of Me